The Great Resignation

and

Quiet Quitting

Why Employees Are Walking Away From Their Jobs

Michael D. Levitt

Breakfast Leadership Network

Published by Breakfast Leadership, LLC

113 W G. Street # 1019

San Diego, CA 92101

BreakfastLeadership.com

Printed in the United States of America

Cover design by Michael D. Levitt

Interior design by Michael D. Levitt

The information contained in this book is intended to be educational and informative. It is not intended to serve as a substitute for professional medical advice or to be used for diagnosing or treating any medical condition. Always consult with your physician or healthcare provider before starting any new diet, exercise program, or healthcare regimen. The author and publisher are not responsible for any adverse effects or consequences resulting from the use of any of the information, suggestions, or procedures described in this book.

Chapter 1: Introduction

Welcome to *The Great Resignation*.

Why are people quitting their jobs at levels that haven't been seen before? My friend, that is a complex answer, which is why I'm happy you acquired this book. The following chapters will identify the complex reasons why The Great Resignation has come to exist, and solutions for employers and employees to address the causes of why people would rather quit and go on their own, than work another minute with their existing company.

When you read stories about people crying in their cars before going to work, you know there's something going on. They don't like the job, their co-workers, or their boss. They don't want to deal with all of the drama that their workplace offers, which impacts their physical and mental health.

The Covid-19 (C-19) pandemic created remote work for many people, which brought to light what I've seen happening for years: employees don't feel free when they're chained to their desks and cubicles.

A Bloomberg News survey in May 2021 indicated that 39% would consider quitting if their employers weren't flexible about remote work. Among millennials and Gen Z, that figure was 49%.

Employers will continue to lose key talent unless they change their habits, beliefs, and antiquated definitions of what "work" is. More on that later.

Sarah Fleming, a freelance photographer from Detroit, quit her job after receiving notice from her employer that she had to return to the office. “I’d rather bet on myself than stay somewhere and be unhappy.”

Commute times suck. I’ve had 90-minute one-way commutes in my career, and even utilized public transit (buses and subways if you don’t have those in your area.), it’s still hours of your day that take a toll on your well-being.

When employees were forced to work remotely, it let a cat out of the bag for many people, that longed for the ability to work remotely. Few employers have a leg to stand on regarding remote work. Many organizations worked just fine with remote employees (spoiler alert: some companies have been using remote workers for a long time.). It boils down to a control tactic by lousy managers and leaders.

Yes, I said it. Lousy managers. What makes a manager lousy?

US News & World Report identifies some traits of bad leaders:

- Micromanaging
- Burned out
- Unprofessional
- Poor communication
- Demanding authority
- Unprepared
- Unapproachable
- Wanting their team to make them look good
- Negative
- Bullying
- Playing favorites
- Doesn’t walk the talk
- Low emotional intelligence
- Assigning blame
- Stealing credit

Does any of these traits sound familiar? My hunch is that you're nodding your head and thinking that this list describes your boss.

Imagine during your interview that the interviewer said these are the qualities of your potential new boss. Would you take the job? Your answer should be a resounding hell no.

47 million Americans quit their jobs in 2021, according to the US Bureau of Labor Statistics. That is a staggering number, since there is 332 million Americans total, and not all of those Americans are of working age. LinkedIn CEO Ryan Roslanksy said this is "unlike anything we've seen. Reasons vary, but some people decided to retire early, and others left their previous jobs due to the pandemic. As our population continues to age, many adults have caregiving responsibilities for their parents and/or children.

To be more effective in alleviating employee burnout, organizations need to reconsider aspects of the work itself instead of just trying to focus on fixing their employees.

In recent months, the workforce has witnessed a new trend that has shaken traditional views on work-life balance and job satisfaction. This trend, known as the "Great Resignation," refers to an increasing number of employees quitting their jobs in record numbers, often without a backup plan. At the same time, there is a quieter trend known as "quiet quitting," in which employees disengage from their work and put in the bare minimum of effort to keep their jobs.

Many questions have been raised about why these phenomena are occurring now and what they mean for the future of work. This chapter will provide an overview of the Great Resignation and quiet quitting, as well as examine the reasons for these trends and the statistical evidence that supports them.

The Great Resignation

The term "Great Resignation" refers to the recent wave of resignations that has hit the workforce, with a significant increase in the number of employees quitting their jobs. Burnout, increased remote work opportunities, a desire for greater work-life balance, and a reevaluation of personal and professional goals in the aftermath of the COVID-19 pandemic have all contributed to this trend.

Quiet Quitting

Quiet quitting, on the other hand, is a more subtle trend that is more difficult to quantify but equally significant. This trend refers to employees who are disengaged and uninterested in their jobs rather than quitting. These employees frequently do the bare minimum to keep their jobs and are uninterested in their work or the company's mission.

Stats Tell The Story

The trends of the Great Resignation and quiet quitting are not just anecdotal but statistically supported. According to the Bureau of Labor Statistics, the US quit rate reached a record high of 4.2 million in June 2021. Furthermore, a Microsoft survey found that 41% of employees were considering leaving their jobs this year, while another Prudential study found that 1 in 4 workers planned to look for a new job when the pandemic ended.

Conclusion: The Great Resignation and quiet quitting are unavoidable trends. They are manifestations of a shifting workforce that prioritizes work-life balance, personal fulfillment, and purpose over traditional career paths. Employers must adapt to retain top talent and attract new employees as more employees take control of their lives and careers. This chapter will offer insights into the causes and consequences of these trends, assisting employers in navigating this new era of work.

Chapter 2: The Reasons Behind The Great Resignation

The term "Great Resignation" refers to the increasing number of people quitting their jobs in various industries around the world. According to a recent Microsoft study, 41% of the global workforce was thinking about leaving their current jobs, and more than half (54%) planned to quit and look for new opportunities in 2022. The impact of the pandemic on employee priorities, work-life balance and flexibility, health concerns and safety measures, economic uncertainty and job security, burnout and stress, and changes in company culture have all been linked to this phenomenon.

The Pandemic's Impact on Employee Priorities

The COVID-19 pandemic has significantly altered how people work, live, and communicate. Employee priorities have shifted as a result. According to a McKinsey & Company study, employees' top priorities are now job security, work-life balance, and meaningful work. They also value working for companies that share their values and care about their well-being. People have become more aware of the importance of their health, family, and personal lives as a result of the pandemic, prompting them to reconsider their work-life balance and job satisfaction.

Flexibility and Work-Life Balance

The pandemic has also heightened the importance of work-life balance and flexibility. Because of the pandemic-induced lockdowns, many employees are working from home, blurring the lines between work and personal life. As a result, people are looking for jobs that provide flexible working hours, remote work, and fewer work-related demands outside of normal working hours. According to a LinkedIn survey, 61% of professionals said work-life balance has become more important to them since the pandemic, with 54% saying they would consider a pay cut for a better work-life balance.

Health Concerns and Safety Precautions

The pandemic has raised concerns about workplace health and safety. People are concerned about their own and the health of who they love, particularly those who are more vulnerable to the virus. Employees have been stressed as a result of the need for safety measures such as masks, social distancing, and vaccination policies. Many employees are looking for jobs that provide a safe and healthy workplace and prioritize employee well-being.

Uncertainty in the Economy and Job Security

The pandemic has created significant economic uncertainty, with many businesses suffering financial losses and reorganizing. As a result, job losses have occurred, and unemployment rates have risen. The pandemic has made people realize the value of job security, and many are looking for jobs that provide a stable work environment as well as opportunities for advancement.

Stress and burnout

Employees have experienced burnout and stress as a result of the pandemic, resulting in a decline in mental and physical health. Many employees have been working long hours, taking on extra responsibilities, and dealing with the pandemic's stress. Burnout and stress have resulted in higher absenteeism, lower productivity, and lower job satisfaction. Many employees are looking for jobs that provide a better work-life balance, rest and recovery opportunities, and supportive work cultures that prioritize employee well-being.

Company Culture Shifts

The pandemic has altered how people work and interact with one another. Many businesses have shifted to remote work, which has resulted in changes in company culture and communication. Remote work has made it more difficult for employees to connect with and interact with coworkers, resulting in a decline in company culture. Employee retention is higher in companies that prioritize employee well-being, foster a positive work culture, and provide opportunities for personal and professional growth.

Conclusion

The Great Resignation is a complex phenomenon caused by a variety of factors. Employee priorities, work-life balance and flexibility, health concerns and safety measures, economic uncertainty and job security, burnout and stress, and changes in company culture have all been impacted by the pandemic. Employers can retain employees by putting employee well-being first and providing a safe and healthy working environment.

Chapter 3: The Impact of The Great Resignation On Employers

The term "Great Resignation," which refers to a mass exodus of employees from their jobs, has become more popular in recent years. Employers are struggling to find and retain talent, while also incurring increased costs associated with hiring and training new employees as a result of this trend. In this chapter, we will look at how the Great Resignation has affected employers, focusing on the difficulty of finding and retaining talent, the increased costs of hiring and training new employees, the need to adapt to changing employee expectations, and the importance of maintaining a positive company culture.

Difficulties in Recruiting and Retaining Talent

The difficulty in finding and retaining talent is one of the most significant effects of the Great Resignation on employers. Employers are left with vacant positions that can be difficult to fill as employees leave their jobs in search of better opportunities. Employers are also facing increased competition for top talent as a result of the pandemic's hiring.

Employers are coming up with novel ways to attract and retain talent in order to address these challenges. Offering more competitive salaries, flexible work arrangements, and robust benefits packages are all part of this. Employers are also investing in employee development programs, career advancement opportunities, and other perks to keep employees on board.

Hiring and training new employees incur additional costs

The increased costs associated with hiring and training new employees is another effect of the Great Resignation on employers. Companies may need to invest in costly recruitment efforts to attract top talent as they try to fill vacant positions. Once hired, new employees must be trained, which can be an expensive process for businesses.

Employers are looking for ways to streamline their recruitment and onboarding processes in order to reduce these costs. Using technology to automate recruitment efforts, collaborating with staffing agencies, and implementing more efficient training programs are all examples of this.

Adapting to Changing Employee Expectations

The Great Resignation has also brought to light the importance of employers adapting to changing employee expectations. Employers must adjust their policies and practises to meet the needs of employees who want more flexibility, work-life balance, and opportunities for advancement.

This includes providing employees with more flexible work arrangements, such as remote work options, as well as opportunities to upskill and reskill. Employers must also prioritize creating a positive work environment that fosters a sense of belonging, purpose, and connection.

Maintaining a Positive Company Culture is Critical

Finally, the Great Resignation has emphasized the importance of preserving a positive corporate culture. Employers must prioritise creating a positive work environment as employees seek companies that align with their values and provide a sense of purpose.

Focusing on employee engagement and satisfaction, fostering open communication, and providing opportunities for professional growth and development are all part of this. Employers must also be transparent, honest, and accountable in their interactions with employees, while also working to foster a culture of trust and respect.

Conclusion

From the difficulty in finding and retaining talent to the increased costs associated with hiring and training new employees, the Great Resignation has had a significant impact on employers. To attract and retain top talent, employers must adapt to changing employee expectations and prioritize maintaining a positive company culture. Companies that invest in their employees can build a strong and resilient workforce that is ready to face the challenges of the post-pandemic world.

Chapter 4: The Role of Technology

Over the last few decades, technology has played a significant role in transforming the way we work. Employees can now work from anywhere, at any time, thanks to the widespread adoption of computers, the internet, and mobile devices. This has resulted in new opportunities for flexibility and autonomy, as well as new challenges for both employees and employers.

The blurring of work and personal life boundaries is one of the most difficult challenges associated with technology in the workplace. It's easy to feel like you're always on the clock with email, messaging apps, and video conferencing tools. This can result in burnout and stress, both of which can contribute to a desire to leave a job.

Employees can now find new job opportunities more easily thanks to advances in technology. It's easier than ever to connect with potential employers and learn about job openings thanks to online job boards, social media, and professional networking sites. Employees can now more easily explore new career paths and find work that matches their values and interests.

The Importance of Remote Work

Because of the COVID-19 pandemic, many employers were forced to adapt to a remote workforce in order to comply with public health guidelines. While remote work has many advantages, such as increased flexibility and reduced commuting time, it also has drawbacks.

Remote work can be isolating, and it can be difficult to stay connected to coworkers and the company culture. This can lead to feelings of disengagement and a lack of motivation, which can influence the decision to quit a job.

The Influence of Automation

The impact of automation is another factor that has contributed to the Great Resignation. By eliminating mundane and repetitive tasks, automation has the potential to transform the workplace, freeing up time for more creative and fulfilling work.

Automation, on the other hand, has the potential to displace workers and create job insecurity. Employees who believe their jobs are in jeopardy are more likely to look for new opportunities, even if they are happy in their current position.

Conclusion

Technology's role in the Great Resignation is complex and multifaceted. While technology has increased employee flexibility and autonomy, it has also introduced new challenges and sources of stress. Employers must recognize the impact of technology on the workplace and take steps to mitigate its negative effects as they navigate this changing landscape. Employers can reduce turnover and retain top talent in a competitive job market by fostering a work-life balance culture, providing opportunities for professional development and growth, and leveraging technology in ways that support employee well-being.

Chapter 5: The Psychology of Quiet Quitting

Quitting is an inevitable part of life. When we quit something that is no longer serving us, it can be a positive experience, but it can also be a negative experience when we feel like we've given up on something important. People are often aware of the benefits of quitting, but they find it difficult to quit because they feel like they're giving up or are concerned about the judgment of others. This chapter will look at the psychology of "quiet quitting," which refers to quitting without making a big announcement or drawing attention to oneself.

In recent years, a new trend in the American labor market has emerged: "quiet quitting." Employees who leave their jobs without giving their employers any notice or explanation are referred to as this phenomenon. Rather than making a dramatic exit, these people simply stop showing up for work or send a brief email to their boss stating that they will not be returning.

According to a recent Accountemps survey, 88% of human resource managers have experienced at least one instance of quiet quitting in their careers. Furthermore, 58% of employees admitted to quitting their jobs without giving notice, up from 48% in 2017.

So, why are an increasing number of people choosing the silent treatment when it comes to quitting their jobs? One reason could be the current tight labor market, in which job seekers have more bargaining power than ever. Workers may feel emboldened to leave their jobs on their own terms as unemployment rates remain low and the number of job openings increases, without fear of burning bridges or damaging their professional reputations.

The prevalence of job-hopping among younger generations is another factor that could be contributing to the rise of quiet quitting. Millennials and

Gen Zers are known for their frequent job changes, with the average millennial changing jobs every two to three years. This constant turnover can make it more difficult for employees to form strong relationships with their managers and coworkers, making it easier to leave quietly.

Whatever the reasons for this trend, quiet quitting can have serious consequences for both employers and employees. Unexpected departures can result in lost productivity, increased costs associated with finding and training replacements, and a drop in employee morale. Individuals who leave a job without giving notice or having a candid conversation with their manager may find it difficult to obtain a positive reference or a potential job offer in the future.

Finally, the rise of quiet quitting is a trend that both employers and employees should be aware of. While it may be tempting to simply walk away from a job without looking back, you must consider the long-term impact on your career and reputation. Employers, too, should take a proactive approach to addressing this trend by cultivating a positive work environment, establishing clear expectations regarding resignation procedures, and being open to feedback and dialogue with their employees.

The Advantages of Quiet Quitting

There are numerous advantages to quitting quietly. For starters, it can help people maintain their self-esteem and self-worth. Individuals who leave quietly are not subject to the scrutiny and judgment of others. This is especially important when they are quitting something important to them, such as a job or a relationship. Individuals can avoid the negative feelings that come with being judged or criticized by quitting quietly.

Another advantage of quitting quietly is that it allows people to focus on their own needs and desires. When we quit something loudly, we are frequently concerned with how others will perceive our decision. When we quit quietly, however, we can focus on what we want and need and make decisions that are in our best interests.

The Quiet Quitting Psychology

Quitting quietly has a complicated psychology. Many factors, including personality traits, past experiences, and cultural norms, can influence an individual's decision to quit quietly.

Personality traits: Some people are more introverted or shy than others, and they may be more likely to leave quietly. These people may prefer to avoid conflict and attention, and they may be hesitant to make a public announcement about their decision to resign.

Past Experiences: An individual's decision to quit quietly may be influenced by past experiences. If a person has had a bad experience quitting loudly in the past, they may be more likely to choose a quieter method in the future. For example, if a person was met with criticism and judgment after quitting a job loudly, they may be hesitant to do so again.

Cultural norms can also influence an individual's decision to leave quietly. Quitting quietly may be more acceptable in some cultures, while making a big announcement when quitting something important may be expected in others.

Overcoming the Fear of Quitting Quietly

Despite the benefits of quitting quietly, many people struggle with the fear of doing so. This fear can be caused by a number of factors, including fear of being judged by others, fear of failure, and fear of the unknown.

Individuals can take a number of steps to overcome their fear of quitting quietly. To begin, they can concentrate on the advantages of quitting quietly, such as maintaining self-esteem and focusing on their own needs. Second, they can remind themselves that their decision to quit is their own and that they have the right to make decisions that are best for them. Finally, they can enlist the assistance of trusted friends, family members, or professionals to guide them through the process.

Conclusion

To summarize, the psychology of quiet quitting is complicated, but it can be beneficial for people who want to focus on their own needs while maintaining their self-esteem. We can better support those who are struggling with this decision if we understand the factors that contribute to an individual's decision to quit quietly. Individuals can overcome their fear of quitting quietly with the right support and mindset and make decisions that are in their best interests.

Chapter 6: Why Employees Are Fighting a Return to the Office

Because of the Covid-19 pandemic, many businesses were forced to transition to remote work, which was a significant change for both employees and employers. With the introduction of vaccines and a decrease in Covid cases, many businesses are planning to reopen. Some employees, however, are resistant to the change and are fighting the return to the office. In this chapter, we will look at the statistics that explain why employees are resisting the return to work.

Covid-19 Fear

Fear of contracting Covid-19 is one of the main reasons why employees are resisting returning to work. According to a Harvard Business School survey, 40% of employees who are hesitant to return to work cite concerns about Covid-19 as their primary reason. A recent study published in the Journal of Occupational and Environmental Medicine found that workers who returned to work during the pandemic were more likely to contract Covid-19.

Increased Adaptability

The increased flexibility that comes with remote work is another reason why employees are resisting the return to the office. According to a FlexJobs survey, 58% of employees who are hesitant to return to the office enjoy the flexibility of remote work. This includes the ability to work from home, set their own schedule, and spend more time with their families.

Time and Cost of Commuting

The commute to work is frequently cited as a major source of stress for employees. According to a Robert Half survey, 34% of employees who are hesitant to return to work cite commuting as the primary reason. The average American commute time is 27.6 minutes each way, amounting to more than 200 hours per year. Furthermore, commuting can be costly, with the average American spending $2,000 per year on commuting expenses.

Increased Productivity

Many employees have discovered that working from home increases their productivity. According to an Owl Labs survey, 71% of remote workers are more productive when working from home. Fewer distractions, a quieter work environment, and the ability to focus without interruptions all contribute to increased productivity.

Work-Life Integration

Finally, many employees are concerned about work-life balance. According to a Buffer survey, 22% of remote workers cite work-life balance as the primary reason for continuing to work remotely. Employees have more control over their schedules and can better balance their work and personal lives with remote work.

Conclusion

The Covid-19 pandemic has significantly altered how and where we work. While some employees are eager to return to work, many are opposed to the change. Employees are fighting the return to the office for a variety of reasons, including fear of Covid-19, increased flexibility, commute time and costs, increased productivity, and work-life balance. Businesses must carefully consider these factors as they plan their return to the office and find ways to accommodate their employees' needs.

Chapter 7: Retaining Talent

Keeping top talent is a critical challenge for businesses today. The ability of a company to retain its best employees can mean the difference between success and failure. Organizations must create a supportive and inclusive workplace culture, provide competitive salaries and benefits, opportunities for professional growth and development, work-life balance and flexibility, and support employee health and well-being to achieve this. In this chapter, we will discuss the significance of these factors in retaining top talent and offer suggestions for creating a culture that encourages employee retention.

Meaningful work is one of the most important factors for employees to be satisfied with their jobs. Meaningful work is work that gives employees a sense of purpose, fulfillment, and engagement while also allowing them to feel like they are making a valuable contribution to their organization and society as a whole. There are several steps you can take as a manager or leader to make work more meaningful for your employees.

Define the Organization's Purpose and Goals Clearly

One of the first steps towards making work more meaningful is to clearly define the purpose and goals of the organization. This includes explaining why the organization exists, what it hopes to accomplish, and how each employee's work contributes to these objectives. Employees are more likely to feel meaningful and important when they understand the big picture.

Make Opportunities for Professional Growth and Development Available

Employees are more likely to find work meaningful if they believe they are professionally growing and developing. Giving employees opportunities for training, mentoring, and career advancement can help them learn new skills and gain new experiences. This can also assist them in seeing how their work fits into a larger career path, which can make it more meaningful.

Encourage Teamwork and Collaboration

Collaboration and teamwork can make employees feel as though they are a part of something bigger than themselves. Employees can develop a sense of camaraderie and shared purpose by working together to achieve common goals. Encouragement of collaboration also allows employees to learn from one another, which can lead to personal and professional growth.

Give Regular Feedback and Acknowledgement

Employees are more likely to find their jobs meaningful if they receive regular feedback and acknowledgement for their efforts. This can be as simple as recognising a job well done or providing constructive feedback to assist employees in improving. Employees can feel valued and appreciated when they receive regular feedback on how their work contributes to the organization's goals.

Make Your Workplace a Happy Place to Work

Creating a positive workplace environment can also help to make work more meaningful. This can include things like creating a trusting and safe physical environment, promoting work-life balance, and fostering a culture of trust and respect. Employees are more likely to find meaning in their work when they feel supported and valued.

Developing a Positive and Inclusive Workplace Culture

Creating a supportive and inclusive workplace culture is one of the most important factors in retaining top talent. Employees who feel valued and included are more likely to stick around. This can be accomplished through a variety of methods, including:

Organizations should actively celebrate diversity and foster an environment in which employees feel comfortable being themselves. This can be accomplished by hosting events that honour various cultures, religions, and backgrounds.

Employers should encourage open communication and feedback in order to ensure that all employees feel heard and valued. This can be accomplished through regular check-ins, town hall meetings, and other forums in which employees can express their ideas and concerns.

Employers should provide support and resources to their employees in order for them to succeed. Mentorship programs, training and development opportunities, and access to technology and tools that allow employees to do their jobs effectively are examples of this.

Providing Competitive Salary and Benefits

Offering competitive salaries and benefits is another important factor in retaining top talent. Employees who believe they are being fairly compensated are more likely to remain with a company. This can be accomplished by:

Salary reviews should be conducted on a regular basis to ensure that employees are paid fairly and competitively. This can help to keep employees from leaving for higher-paying positions.

Employers should provide comprehensive benefits packages that include health insurance, retirement plans, and other perks that employees value.

Providing Opportunities for Professional Development and Growth

Another important factor in retaining top talent is providing opportunities for professional growth and development. Employees who believe they have opportunities to learn and grow are more likely to remain with a company. This can be accomplished by:

Employers should provide training and development programs that assist employees in developing their skills and knowledge. Workshops, online courses, and mentoring programs are examples of this.

Opportunities for advancement: Employers should provide opportunities for advancement to employees who have demonstrated their ability to perform well. Promotions, transfers to other departments, and leadership positions are examples of this.

Maintaining Work-Life Flexibility and Balance

Work-life balance and flexibility are becoming more important in retaining top talent. Employees who believe they have a good work-life balance and the ability to work flexibly are more likely to stay with a company. This can be accomplished by:

Employers should provide flexible working arrangements, such as remote work or flexible schedules, to help employees achieve a healthy work-life balance.

Time off: To help employees recharge and balance their personal and professional lives, employers should provide generous time off policies such as vacation time, sick leave, and parental leave.

Employee Health and Well-Being Support

Employee health and well-being are critical to the success of any organization. Employees who are healthy and happy are more productive, engaged, and committed to their jobs. It is your responsibility as an employer to create an environment that promotes your employees' physical, mental, and emotional health. In this article, we will look at some of the ways you can help employees with their health and well-being.

Make Your Workplace Safe and Healthy

Employee well-being is built on a safe and healthy work environment. You must ensure that your workplace is clean, well-lit, and well-ventilated as an employer. You should also provide ergonomic furniture and equipment to your employees to reduce the risk of injury or strain. Regular workplace maintenance, including cleaning and sanitization, is critical to preventing the spread of infectious diseases.

Promote Physical Activity

Sedentary work environments can result in a variety of health issues, such as obesity, heart disease, and diabetes. Encourage physical activity among your employees as a means of improving their health and well-being. This can be accomplished by providing on-site fitness facilities, offering incentives to employees who participate in physical activity programs or encouraging employees to walk or cycle to work.

Make Healthy Food Options Available

Employees' health and well-being can be greatly influenced by the food they consume. Healthy food options, such as fresh fruits and vegetables, whole grains, and lean proteins, can help to lower the risk of chronic diseases and improve overall health. You can accomplish this by providing healthy snacks and meals in the workplace, or by collaborating with local restaurants or caterers that provide healthy options.

Mental Health Guidance

Physical and mental health are equally important. Stress, anxiety, and depression are all common mental health issues that can negatively impact employee well-being and productivity. As an employer, you can promote mental health by providing access to counseling services, stress-management workshops, and mental health resources and information.

Encourage Work-Life Integration

A balance between work and personal life is critical for employee well-being. Encourage employees to take breaks, use vacation time, and avoid working long hours to reduce stress and burnout. You can also provide employees with flexible work arrangements, such as telecommuting or flexible work schedules, to help them balance their work and personal responsibilities.

Employees Should Be Recognized and Rewarded

Recognizing and rewarding employees for their efforts and accomplishments is an important way to contribute to their well-being. Employees can be motivated and satisfied with positive feedback, bonuses, and incentives. Recognizing employees for their contributions can also help to foster a positive work culture and foster an employee sense of community.

Finally, supporting employee health and well-being is critical for any organization's success. You can create a workplace that promotes employee health and well-being by providing a safe and healthy work environment, encouraging physical activity, offering healthy food options, supporting mental health, encouraging work-life balance, and recognising and rewarding employees.

To summarize, making work meaningful for employees is a critical component of creating a positive and productive workplace. Managers and leaders can help employees find meaning and purpose in their work by clearly defining the organization's purpose and goals, providing opportunities for professional growth and development, encouraging collaboration and teamwork, providing regular feedback and recognition, and creating a positive work environment.

Chapter 8: How Employees Can Navigate The Great Resignation

The Great Resignation caused many employees to reconsider their careers, values, and priorities. According to a Microsoft survey, 41% of employees plan to leave their current jobs within the next year. This chapter outlines strategies for employees to use during the Great Resignation.

Identifying Personal Values and Priorities

Identifying personal priorities and values is the first step in navigating the Great Resignation. Employees should consider what matters most to them, such as work-life balance, job security, career advancement, financial stability, and mental health. Employees can make more informed career decisions if they understand their priorities and values.

Negotiating for Higher Pay and Benefits

As companies struggle to retain employees, many are increasing employee compensation and benefits. Employees should be proactive in negotiating better pay and benefits, particularly if they have specialized skills or experience. Negotiating for higher pay and benefits necessitates planning, research, and confidence. Employees should be prepared to argue why they deserve a raise or better benefits based on their performance, market demand for their skills, and the financial performance of the company.

Seeking Opportunities for Professional Development and Growth

Employees can also navigate the Great Resignation by looking for opportunities for professional growth and development. This can include furthering one's education or training, volunteering for new projects or committees, or seeking mentorship from more experienced colleagues. Professional development and growth can assist employees in remaining engaged in their work, developing new skills, and positioning themselves for future career opportunities.

Keeping a Healthy Work-Life Balance

Balancing work and life is one of the Great Resignation's challenges. Employees should prioritize a healthy work-life balance by setting boundaries, taking breaks, and practicing self-care. Taking time off, delegating responsibilities, and disconnecting from work during off-hours are all examples of this. Maintaining a healthy work-life balance can assist employees in avoiding burnout, increasing productivity and job satisfaction, and maintaining positive relationships with coworkers and loved ones.

Creating a Support Network

Finally, employees should create a support network to help them navigate the Great Resignation's challenges. Friends, family members, colleagues, and mentors can all offer emotional support, advice, and resources. Creating a support network can also assist employees in remaining connected to their industry and discovering new career opportunities.

Conclusion

Employees face both challenges and opportunities as a result of the Great Resignation. Employees can navigate this period of uncertainty and position themselves for long-term career success by identifying personal priorities and values, negotiating for better compensation and benefits, seeking opportunities for professional growth and development, maintaining a healthy work-life balance, and developing a support network.

Chapter 9: Conclusion

The Great Resignation and Quiet Quitting have unmistakably left their imprint on the employment landscape. The nature of work and the relationships between employees and employers have been fundamentally altered as workers navigate the uncertain terrain of a post-pandemic world. As we near the end of this book, it is important to consider the long-term implications of these trends and make predictions for the future of work.

The Great Resignation has highlighted issues that have been simmering for years. Workers want more autonomy, a better work-life balance, and more meaningful work. The pandemic has demonstrated that old ways of working are no longer adequate, and that employers must adapt in order to attract and retain talent. As workers continue to vote with their feet, we can expect to see a continued shift towards flexible work arrangements and a focus on workplace well-being.

Simultaneously, the rise of Quiet Quitting suggests that many workers are simply opting out of traditional employment entirely. These workers seek greater control over their careers and lives, whether through freelancing, entrepreneurship, or other non-traditional paths. This trend may result in a more diverse and dynamic economy, but it also poses difficulties for employers who must compete for talent in an increasingly crowded market.

In the future, it is clear that hybrid work environments will play a significant role. Because of the pandemic, many workers have come to prefer the flexibility and autonomy that remote work provides. Simultaneously, there is a desire for social connection and collaboration that can only be achieved in person. As a result, hybrid work models that combine the best of both worlds are becoming more common.

Employers will need to be more responsive to their employees' needs and desires in this new landscape. Offering more flexible work arrangements, investing in employee well-being, and cultivating a culture of trust and transparency are all examples of how this can be accomplished. It will also necessitate adaptability to new technologies and changing market conditions.

Overall, the Great Resignation and Quiet Quitting mark a watershed moment in labour history. The old ways of doing things are clearly no longer sustainable as workers demand more from their employers and seek greater control over their careers. The future of work will be defined by flexibility, autonomy, and a focus on well-being, and employers who can adapt to these new realities will thrive in the coming years.

~

Are you looking for ways to prevent burnout and lower the chances of your employees quitting quietly or joining the great resignation trend? The Breakfast Leadership Network is the answer!

We provide a variety of services designed specifically to assist organizations in confronting these issues. Our burnout prevention program includes a thorough assessment of your workplace culture and stressors, as well as tailored coaching and training sessions to provide your leaders and employees with the tools they need to manage stress and avoid burnout.

Our strategy also aims to prevent quiet quitting, which occurs when employees become disengaged and mentally check out without leaving their job. We offer strategies for identifying and addressing these issues, resulting in higher levels of employee satisfaction and retention.

Finally, as the great resignation trend looms, we are here to assist organizations in proactively addressing any underlying issues that may cause employees to leave. Our expert team advises on employee engagement, leadership development, and workplace culture to ensure that your organization is a place where employees feel valued, supported, and motivated to stay for the long term.

Don't put it off until it's too late! Contact Breakfast Leadership today to learn more about how we can help you avoid burnout, quiet quitting, and the Great Resignation. Visit BreakfastLeadership.com.

Printed in Great Britain
by Amazon

30098518R00020